Cover Image Used by Permission (Leah Hogsten | The Salt Lake Tribune)
Members of the First Presidency of The Church of Jesus Christ of Latter-day
Saints, from left, Dallin H. Oaks, Russell M. Nelson and Henry B. Eyring lead
the spring General Conference Saturday, April 1, 2023.

https://www.sltrib.com/opinion/commentary/2023/06/02/james-sawyer-
saving-when-mormons/

James E. Sawyer, Emeritus, Seattle University

Access to Some Links May Incur Charges

For Linda

CONTENTS

CHAPTER 1: GARGOYLES AND OTHER CREEPY STUFF

YO MITT:

Thanks for your new metaphor about authoritarianism: that it's like creepy gargoyles lurking from the rooftops of medieval cathedrals. I like it, really. I picked it up from Michelle Goldberg, *New York Times*, who cites your biographer McKay Coppins.

But I wonder, Mitt. How about adding moral turpitude type behaviors such as bullying—to the authoritarian mix you mention? And, what about sprinkling in some "dark religion" in order to portray Utah's situation authentically?

Of course, with bullying and beyond, 2024 is likely to be a scary, gargoyle-infested year. So, I wonder. Rather than shunning them, why not inject gargoyles at every turn—at least metaphorically —into America's sometimes ungodly political and cultural mix. Culture war be damned, some might say! Especially, let's rely on gargoyles to remind us of forthcoming election year hacks—even those in progress as we head toward election day, November 5, and beyond.

I'm keying off David Von Drehle, Michelle Goldberg's *NYT* colleague, who offers useful ideas about authoritarianism and conformity, perhaps with some obscure gargoyle-like connections. Von Drehle speaks of America's epidemic of discouragement; that it's rooted in a mistaken vision of American exceptionalism.

The cultural right, Von Drehle observes, is nostalgic for a past that never existed, with a vision of a homogeneous nation—also nonexistent—linked with prior success claims—highly overamped—of bountiful American peace and prosperity outcomes. In Von Drehle's view, it's an alt-right pipe dream about who prior Americans have been, as well as who contemporary Americans are becoming.

Is Von Drehle's assessment true, Mitt? If so, then shouldn't MAGA and other Republicans recalibrate erroneous visions of America's past, even as they begin—hopefully—seeking accommodation with moderates and liberals—to craft visions of a future that's aspirational—not just for some, but for all Americans?

Goldberg claims that you, Mitt, are unimpressed with Joe Biden's first-of-the-new-year speech from Pennsylvania's hallowed Valley Forge, about J6 insurrection at our nation's capital, three years ago. Stop kicking a dead political horse, you say. Biden should find some new material, you say. Is this true?

Deceased Mormon President Spencer Kimball celebrated Mormon conformity. Do you agree, Mitt, or has Kimball's authoritarian legacy become just another "dead-horse-to-not-kick" story?

If strict cultural conformity can be abandoned, even by right-wing Mormon conservatives, then isn't it time to begin working across the political divide, in Utah and beyond? Isn't this a crucial juncture at which to begin building a collaborative America, rather than the democratically dysfunctional, combative one the Republican Party has been assembling?

Hey, what if Mormondom—the term I use to describe the wider cultural context in which Utah has operated since its 1847 settlement—could somehow upend aspects of its dysfunctional conformity by kicking its authoritarian gargoyles down the road —so to speak? Or by sticking them under the rug, or whatever. What think you, Mitt, of such dead-horse-kicking, under-the-rug-sweeping, authoritarian diminishing, Mormondom-leaning scenarios?

While gargoyles were intended originally to ward off evil spirits, their very presence can instill vulnerability and fear. I know. In my Mormondom-conforming family, authoritarianism and moral turpitude-like behaviors appear far too frequently, beginning with shunning that ends too often with bullying. That's the intent and the strategy of perpetrators, I suppose.

So, Mitt, I have a proposal, altered a bit from wherever your gargoyle metaphor might be leading. How about, rather than gargoyles swooping down from Catholic cathedrals, could we envision instead, gargoyles swooping down from the rooftops of Mormon temples? Of course, it could become a little messy up there, what with the high-flying rooftop preeminence of that gilded Mormon angel, Moroni!

Heck. What if we just cut to the chase and imagine gargoyles attacking Latter-day Saints everywhere, starting in Provo, Utah, for instance, all the way to our nation's capital? But should we not add evangelicals, also? And how about alt-right Catholics? And on and on. What say you, Mitt, about including such a huge chunk of the USA, swallowed up, so to speak, even into the fairyland-type belief systems of the alt-right?

Well, Perhaps I'm getting a bit overzealous about your gargoyle thing. But I do stand on this observation. Over more than a century, Mormon Utah has evolved as a hotbed of political dysfunction. The State is not altogether dissimilar from other alt-right-leaning enclaves, I suppose. Still, it's been ongoing since inception in 1847, I believe. And I sense paranoia and political dysfunction seeping out of contemporary places such as Provo and Logan, even to encompass the length and breadth of our cherished American landscape.

Indeed, I claim that to fix America's culture wars, our country needs to self-renew, and why not start with Mormon Utah's oft-dysfunctional, authoritarian culture? It makes sense because culture war-type dysfunction goes back over a century. My state of origin is a place near and dear to our hearts, of course, but one that often fails miserably, due to its inability to sustain basic principles of humanism—decade after decade—creepy gargoyles notwithstanding.

For instance, I'm writing in the moment at the beginning of the Utah State Legislature's 2024 session. Accordingly, the *Salt Lake Tribune* chronicled some early proposals percolating through the Mormon-Republican-dominant legislative process. Utah's is the shortest legislative calendar among the 50 states. And because the Republican Party holds a super-majority, whenever strict party-line votes are taken, proposals initiated by Democrats are unlikely to prevail, ever! Pretty much, Republicans can get whatever they want, mostly, without across-the-aisle collaboration with Democrats. That's what red-state super-majorities are about.

One early Republican bill disallows Utah students—based only on sex as determined at birth, from entering bathrooms and locker rooms designated for the opposite sex. It's designed to impede trans-sexualism. Its designed, also, allegedly, to "lib-flip" those who view trans-sexualism as a far-lesser evil in Utah than some darker Republican-dominated politicking strategies. Another proposed bill would ban public schools and colleges from asking job applicants about their sentiments regarding education-oriented diversity initiatives.

Beyond Utah, similar bills have been moving through other Red state legislative pipelines, circa 2024.

Yet another bill proposal—that failed—was sponsored by Representative Trevor Lee, R-Layton. According to the *Salt Lake Tribune*, Lee's constitutional amendment-oriented language showed up online, a few days prior to the session's January start. Accordingly, a *Tribune* headline decreed "Lawmaker weighs barring immigrant children from public schools." The *Tribune* then explained that Lee's legislative proposal was removed, but it reposted the story the following day, this time with amended text that "condemns the federal government for not responding appropriately to the crisis of illegal immigration."

Lee told the *Tribune* he never intended that his proposed legislation would become a state constitutional amendment—at least in the moment—and that the legislative staff drafted it wrong. However, House Minority Leader Angela Romero, D-Salt Lake, pushed back on Lee's claim, praising the professionalism of nonpartisan legislative staff, and declaring: "There's a process that we follow, and nobody's bill would be put out there publicly, ... [the] elected official would have had to approve it."

The *Tribune's* editorial board cautioned legislators near the beginning of 2024, to avoid spending limited time on culture warfare-type issues such as Lee's, that would ban children of noncitizens from public education, or limit school bathroom access, or put the kibosh on education diversity, and on and on. Instead, the *Tribune* implores elected officials to tackle the momentous problems Utahns face. At the head of the list should be the withering ecology of the Great Salt Lake. The lake continues to be threatened by Utah's over-zealous, short-term oriented, economic development culture, although economic developers may disagree with my assessment.

Mitt, how could legislative tussles such as these be considered prudent utilizations of Utah's legislative calendar? Don't these harbor, instead, miscarriages of democratic process? Can't Utah's public institutions decide these sorts of things on their own, without political bullying by the legislative supermajority? For instance, in Catholic social teaching, one of its aspirational benchmarks is known as the principle of subsidiarity. It holds that social and political issues should be dealt with at the most immediate level, consistent with their resolution.

Anyway, I have a proposal to help fix these Utah sorts of largely religion-inspired chicaneries. I'm calling for a new state mantra. Please tell me what you think, Mitt? It's called "Fix Utah First!" That's right, and I believe in it, passionately.

Ideologically, Utah has been "off the mark" for over a century, I assert. Culture warfare has been evolving in the state, even though many decades ago it didn't amount to much of a problem in many states now designated politically as red. Now, of course, culture war is tying our entire nation in knots.

If Utah could just fix itself—first—by dealing with its authoritarian gargoyles—then I believe it could become a beacon for other states. That's right. I believe Utah could become a leader in moving our nation away from spirit-numbing, bifurcating, war-torn-like, culture-based politics.

Thus, I propose this: Fix Utah First!

Great bumper sticker, eh?

Thanks for listening, or not, Mitt. I'm sure you're eager to go-to-bat for political and religious outliers like me. Right? Maybe? Not so much? Whatever.

I wonder, also. What if the Goldberg-Von Drehle *NYT* duo might consider accepting a gargoyle-enhanced, Utah-based article? You know, one about how to retire authoritarian gargoyles originating in the Mormon-dominant state? If so, might you care to join me as co-author?

Probably not interested, I presume? Not to worry. Anyway, I'm mostly steering clear of Utah and digging in around the much more rational state of my domicile: Colorado. On a whim, however, I might be tempted to move to Jackson Hole. It's the Wyoming home, you know, of that world-class democracy advocate—who I adopted in 2023 as one of my heroes—now-deposed Republican Congresswoman Liz Cheney.

CHAPTER 2: WHY THIS ELECTRONIC BOOKLET? WHY NOW?

Originally, I was an Ogden guy. *YO MITT: MISFEASANCE IN MORMONDOM?* is my memoir-based compendium about historical bullying in Utah and its link to America's contemporary culture wars. And there's more.

I grew up in a crazy sort of mixed-religion family, Mitt, I served a proselyting mission for the Mormon church, worked as special assistant to a Utah governor, completed a PhD in economics, and then departed for an academic career, mostly in the Pacific Northwest, after walking away from a position offered by the Nixon White House.

Two bullying illustrations remain "bright" for me, even now. One pertained to a supervisor, during my part-time, eighth grade newspaper delivery job of Salt Lake's secular newspaper, *The Tribune*. As I went house to house by bike, I collected as well as delivered in an Ogden neighborhood a couple of miles from my family's home.

The other illustration occurred as I watched and worked in the Utah governor's office. In my mid-20s, the institutional Mormon church seemed all-powerful, even as I observed it facing off then—in a civil way, mostly—with Utah moderates and liberals.

My boss, the governor's chief of staff in Cal Rampton's Democratic administration, would schedule occasional closed-door meetings at 47 East South Temple. That's the address the Church of Jesus Christ of Latter-day Saints used then as its administrative headquarters.

Rather than waiting to see if church representatives would make appearances "on the hill," the governor's chief of staff would schedule occasional meetings to ascertain what the institutional church wanted from Utah's government. When I became aware of what I considered to be clandestine meetings, however, I blanched at the appearance that the democratic process was being breached.

When only the big and powerful receive such special audiences, "the system" tilts to favor the big and the powerful.

Regarding my part-time newspaper delivery and collection job, I was earning money—at thirteen—to attend the national Boy Scout Jamboree in Valley Forge, Pennsylvania. A friend told me he was vacating his route and asked if I would like to take it over, which I did. Then, as my departure to Valley Forge grew near, I found another friend to assume the route. All accounts were paid up and I was in good stead with the supervisor at my departure time as I headed for three weeks of scout jamboree and travel.

A few weeks after returning however, I took a disturbing, bully-oriented call from the independently employed supervisor. On that afternoon I was helping my dad at his small store. The caller seemed little interested in the quality and reliability of the work I had performed under his indirect supervision. Instead, he zeroed in on why I handed off the route to a successor without first soliciting his approval.

First off, I explained I handed off to the new guy in precisely the way my predecessor handed off to me. I found a replacement, even as the prior carrier had found me. No supervisory consultation was undertaken.

Then, as his call roared to conclusion, he ended with this parting shot. "You will never amount to anything," he declared. Those were weighty words, coming from someone over three times my age who was also known as the youth leader in a Mormon ward adjacent to where my family lived.

Looking back, I recognize his call was about bullying, apparently because he saw my actions as ego-threatening to him. Rather than recoiling in hurt and fear however, I decided to use his disparaging language as a motivator and a steppingstone.

"I'll show him by living a together, mature life," I thought to myself, at thirteen. And where had I learned to take that sort of stand? It was through attendance at the Mormon church. Consequently, his clandestine call became something of a "leg up" motivator, in my youthful progression that culminated, in my early 30's, with a doctorate.

◆ ◆ ◆

Back to you, Mitt.

For decades I've been impressed with the Romney family, and with your service-oriented career, particularly. That includes sojourns as Utah senator, governor of Massachusetts, organizing committee president of the 2002 Salt Lake Winter Olympics, and of course, volunteer gigs in Boston as Mormon bishop and stake president. Wow!

Wherever you go next, as your Senate term rolls to completion, I anticipate you'll continue fulfilling your family's well-honed trademark of revered public service. No wonder the *Washington Post* ran a commentary recommending you for the Harvard University presidency.

Rest assured; I believe our world needs more Mitt Romneys. And since you're one of my public heroes—as is Liz Cheney— I'm making your service-oriented career the putative focus of this memoir, although at times you might feel I'm treating you flippantly.

Thus said, the cover's photo gives my project away, somewhat. You're familiar, of course, with the threesome. They're the

LDS First Presidency—three noteworthy guys—also committed to public service—but carrying baggage, including an average age of ninety-four. No spring chickens!

The photo, used by permission, comes from Spring General Conference, April 1, 2023 (Leah Hogsten | *The Salt Lake Tribune*). It ran with my June 2, 2023, *Salt Lake Tribune* commentary about alleged institutional "rat-holing" of untaxed tithing dollars rather than for those funds to have been used in entirety for humanitarian and related purposes. My commentary is Saving for When Latter-day Saints Run the World?

LDS church membership, of course, confers specific benefits upon faithful contributors. Those who tithe are rewarded with tax breaks via membership in a huge nonprofit organization for which various allegiances are expected. It is an organization that has grown to hold net assets valued in the hundreds of billion dollars.

A related observation—spilling out of my *Tribune* commentary —is this. Mormons—along with other nonprofit organizations, churches included—ought to carefully avoid marketing their "beliefs" as "knowns," if they are not. In this regard, please note comments—in my *Tribune* commentary, link above—related to philosopher of science Karl Popper.

In a vein related to Popper, Gordon Monson, columnist for the *Salt Lake Tribune,* does a less formal but pretty good job distinguishing between what it means to know, and what it means to merely believe.

For instance, Mormon missionary door approaches that focus on "I know the things I am speaking are true,"—sometimes called testimony bearing—tend to be inappropriate. That's because truthfulness claims made publicly are not amenable—typically —to the criterion Professor Popper describes. That is, any publicly promulgated knowledge claim must be susceptible to invalidation, when invalidation becomes essential. Invalidation of a proposition is only possible if evidence for and against can be assessed objectively, not subjectively.

Consequently, a door approach may be a valid expression of belief when made publicly, but as such, it is not a "known." In most cases, "I believe" is intellectually respectable, whereas "I know" is not, when speaking in public venues such as front porches or school board meetings.

Related also—for the three churchmen pictured—and for all of us —is this. Humility is a crucial attribute. Arrogance should find no place in any church-based messaging, Mormon or otherwise.

So, there you have it. My memoir salutes public service—yours specifically—even as it cautions against conflating "believing" with "knowing." This is not a callout, Mitt, for you to become humble. I don't believe public arrogance characterizes who you are.

My short bio is below. Allegedly, I have acquired some vital experience—over a professional lifetime—that is ability-enhancing regarding discernment about what's real, and what's mere belief. Everyone ought to rise toward a heightened level of discernment about claims of knowing, and to differentiate them thoughtfully from claims of mere believing. This is true especially when pronouncements are made in public spaces, where some listeners to our "shtik" or gimmick may not agree with us.

Jim Sawyer (James E) holds a Ph.D. in labor economics and is professor emeritus from a Jesuit-sponsored university. In Europe, Sawyer was recipient of Fulbright fellowships in France and Portugal, and jointly appointed with a French University.

Sawyer's scholarship focuses on why paradigms fail—in economics, particularly. At Seattle University, leadership assignments included director of the Institute of Public Service, chairperson of the Department of Political Science and Public

Administration, and holder of the Reverend Louis Gaffney, S.J. (endowed) Chair, at times referred to casually as a chair in ethics.

So, Mitt, here's a "big picture precis" of this whole shebang.

First off, this electronic booklet is a proposal for how to end America's culture wars, by starting first—with Utah—and individually—with each of us—rather than to search for the locus of problems outside of us, such as in the lives of "others." Perhaps, we may even go so far—erroneously—as to consider "others" as the enemy.

Good ole' Utah. The state known originally, via beehive symbolism, as the Territory of Deseret, where culture warfare has been raging—I assert—almost from the beginning—when Mormon pioneers entered the Salt Lake Valley in 1847.

This is a simmering conflict—mostly—rather than one of open warfare. Authoritarian bullying limps along, mostly, then at times it boils over. I believe some clandestine aspects of Utah's 45-day, 2024 legislative session are evidence of such a "bullying boil over," and this year it has related especially to the forthcoming presidential election.

Being recipients of someone else's bullying behavior is not new to my family, historically. I also make the distinction between "hard" and "soft" bullying, because I believe soft bullying operates more frequently and often much more subtly, for instance, allegedly, through promulgation of certain edicts authored by the Church of Jesus Christ of Latter-Day Saints.

In the early decades of the Twentieth Century, my father was heavily impacted by hard and soft bullying. As such, he suffered. As I grew to maturity—to a somewhat lesser degree than Buss —I suffered also. My paperboy delivery narrative is such an illustration. I could add others—many others.

This electronic booklet relies upon many Utah-related illustrations. Often, these are connected to Mormondom, which is my term of choice, used to describe the larger milieu impacting Utah Mormons and non-Mormons, alike.

Buss resented the constraints he felt from being stuffed into Utah's Mormon-dominant authoritarian conformity. I am somewhat like him in various ways, but different in others.

I vividly recall the day I received a mission call to New Zealand. Although Buss did not tell me to not go, he did present what he considered to be damning evidence against claims of the Church of Jesus Christ of Latter-day Saints. Buss belonged to the Masonic order, and he claimed members of his order, functioning in mid-nineteenth century Illinois, were among those who martyred the Mormon prophet, Joseph Smith—who also was a member of the Masonic order. Smith's preeminent fault, Buss claimed, was that he blasphemously expropriated Masonic ceremonies and symbols and turned them into Mormon temple rites. Masonic ceremonies and symbols were never intended to be made into religion, he extolled.

I did go to New Zealand for the Mormon church, and it did prove to be one among other life-defining experiences for me. Buss's letters—the only ones I received consistently—sustained me throughout. In our written dialogue, we focused not so much on the veracity of knowledge-based LDS truth claims, but upon opportunities for service to the people of New Zealand who I came to love dearly.

During this period, leadership and motivation of others came easily. At the time I left New Zealand, I was one of a half-dozen supervisors of other missionaries in our North Island jurisdiction.

All told, I both gave and received. As recipient of the ample benefits of Mormon missionary service, I've discovered that some professional "positives" have accumulated more readily for me, due in part to the largely Mormon route I took toward adulthood. I'm far less certain however that a similar route would work well for contemporary adolescents just now navigating challenging life passages through the Mormon "pipeline."

Three years after returning from New Zealand to Utah, I was recruited to serve as special assistant to Utah's governor. As time passed, I found various missionary-related experiences were contributory to my professorial career success. Those also helped me prepare—indirectly—so I could "show well" in vetting processes—FBI vetting included, related to having been recruited to fill a leadership and management position in the Nixon White House.

I remember feeling bullied by a member of President Richard Nixon's inner circle, unfortunately. It occurred in a final White House interview with my much more senior "handler," whose parting "shot" was this. "If you don't accept this job, you'll never amount to anything." It reminded me of being thirteen again, when I was bullied by a supervisor for the *Salt Lake Tribune*.

The occasion was my notification—to the White House—of "regrets." I submitted it even as my pending approval to hold the job was moving through the Congressional pipeline pending confirmation via the Senate Committee on Labor. I chose wisely, I believe. Months later, Nixon was "busted" in the Watergate break in investigation.

CHAPTER 3: SLAMMED BY FAMILY, MAGA STYLE?

YO MITT:

The Salt Lake Tribune continues to remind legislators of the gravity of Utah's situation. Even Brigham Young University's College of Life Sciences warns that emergency measures are needed to save the Great Salt Lake from ecological collapse. Legislatively, however, nothing on the scale of "avoiding collapse" was forthcoming by the time the 2024 legislative session wrapped up on March 1.

Instead, Utah Republican legislators continue to be hell-bent on their "Own the Libs"-type strategy, apparently coordinated with culture warfare strategies in other red states. My hypothesis? There's a direct link, I believe, between America's ongoing culture war crisis, and the genesis of Utah's version of that crisis that dates back many decades.

I'm still very much a Utah guy, Mitt, especially until I exited the state to pursue an academic career, which brings me to my "take" about the nexus of government—and culture—in Utah.

My tenure with Governor Calvin Rampton began in the month of America's manned lunar landing. I watched part of the moonwalk in the company of other statehouse staffers—and Rampton—in his private capitol study. It was Summer, 1969.

Life seemed "on track," but my career was causing high anxiety for my all-conservative family. At about the six-month mark with Rampton, I took a call one morning from Aunt Leona. She said Uncle Myron, visiting Ogden from Los Angeles, was on his way to

Salt Lake City to see me, and then she hung up abruptly.

Soon, I realized that Melba was ringleader in what was fast becoming a weird family stunt, about to boil over. Planning for the fiasco was being executed by three of my maternal grandparents' six children: Myron, Leona, and of course, Melba, my mother.

Even in my mid-20's, mother's family called me Jimmy, my nickname from childhood. For Melba, particularly, sometimes her anger would predispose her to call me, thus: the little loudmouth. It fit my extended maternal family's perception of me as an extraverted dunce. Whereas Melba skipped two school grades and graduated at 15, I had a much slower adolescent take off. Eventually however, I caught up quickly and then began hitting my stride, but without the overhang of bipolarity that afflicted Melba. As I matured, I learned how to capitalize on my unique characteristic: dyslexia. "Connecting the dots" came easily.

I won a national competition in public speaking during my college freshman year. Timewise, Mitt, it occurred as I was challenging my professor in macroeconomics, urging him to acknowledge the "saving-investment equality" is as much an ideological proposition as an empirical one. Years later, my thesis matured into a treatise. My London publisher was the same one Cambridge scholar JM Keynes used, who also advised, informally, on America's economic policies during the Franklin Roosevelt Administration.

Even now, I continue to argue that failure of economists to grapple effectively with disequilibrium leaves the profession underprepared to deal effectively with all sorts of rip-offs, scams, and frauds. It's an argument analogous to Keynes' depression-era argument that an appropriate response to economic dysfunction requires a disequilibrium perspective and response, and not merely a static one.

Keynes' argument is contained in his General Theory. A nonacademic restatement of a Keynes-related disequilibrium perspective is contained in my 2023 public education pamphlet: "What If Republicans Are Dead Wrong About Woke Capitalism?"

College-wise, I completed a degree in psychology, and then signed on with Ogden's municipality and its community action agency to lead remedial programs for poor high school dropouts, called the Neighborhood Youth Corps. I served as a counselor as well as the administrator. Following that, I landed a national internship co-sponsored by the US Department of Labor. And then I landed back in the beehive state, leading initiatives in labor market program development for Governor Rampton.

Once relocated, the threesome of my mother and two of her siblings hatched a plot to "get Jimmy," although it seemed crude and almost hilarious at the time. What was not at all comical, however, was that Utah's chief executive could have been swept up—along with me—in their craziness, had the threesome—along with Myron's wife—been able to fully execute their plot.

This is how their chicanery unfolded. Myron arrived with Marjorie in their black limousine. I presumed they had come for a guided tour of the Utah capitol building, reminiscent of when Myron's father—and my grandfather—worked for Utah's first Democratic governor, German-Jewish immigrant Simon Bamberger, five decades before. That's not what Myron intended, however.

I greeted Uncle Mike and Aunt Marge in the governor's office vestibule, from where I planned to escort them to my office, or so I thought. Remarkably, spontaneously, and without making direct eye contact, or even extending a greeting, the duo launched spontaneously into a funky song- and-dance routine. Right then. Right there.

Septuagenarians from my family, having relocated from Utah to Los Angeles decades before, now were carrying on as adolescents in the executive offices of Utah's governor!

As Mike and Marge paraded about in animated, circular fashion, they chanted in unison—over and over—"Feeding at the trough!

Feeding at the trough!" Then, their little drama of perhaps two or three minutes wound up as quickly as it started, with my aging relatives exiting without even communicating or looking at me directly. Very strange!

Among their implicit, not-so-subtle messages was that I was a "kept man," they asserted, in the thrall of liberal politicians, and causing more harm than good by running remedial labor market programs, funded by President Lyndon Johnson's War on Poverty. A colleague, standing nearby, asked "What was that about?" And I responded as we returned to our offices: "Nothing much; those are just two of my crazy relatives."

Later, I reflected. Why me? What did Mother's family want? Did Uncle Mike figure he was settling some sort of family score, vis-à-vis my job? Or was he driven by some unfulfilled, adolescent-type grudge, harbored vis-à-vis his deceased father, Charles?

Grandfather Charles died three years before I was born. I wish I could have known him. He was an early graduate, circa 1895, of Logan's Utah State University, and then he took his first job as a teacher in the rural enclave of Morgan County, where the Condie family resided. Across his truncated life, Charles led a remarkable public service career. In addition to school headmaster in Morgan, he served as Morgan County Attorney, water commissioner for the agricultural "life blood" Weber and Ogden rivers, and as chairperson of the Morgan County Republican Party for two decades. But that was not all.

Government work was ill regarded in Morgan, as well as throughout much of the ideologically conservative domains of rural Utah, then and now. Charles's government career evolved, in line with the evolution of America's progressive era, about the time World War I raged on the European continent. Progressivism, as it was known, was associated with the upscaling of government programs and services to meet the demands of early-Twentieth-Century urbanization. Consequently, not only was "enhanced government" received in an unpopular manner by

Mormon rural-dwellers, but also by any and all Utahns favoring minimalist government philosophies, known as laissez-fare.

Eventually, Charles found himself living and working in Salt Lake City, about 30 miles west of Morgan. He had signed on temporarily with Democrats as Utah's director of weights and measures. His job was to create and maintain a regulatory structure for verifying that a gallon of gasoline in Logan would be precisely the same measure as a gallon sold on the streets of Salt Lake City or anywhere else throughout the state.

Commercial and industrial standardization was crucial to our nation's economic development. Way beyond mere gasoline, of course, this manifestation of Charles's career was anathema to conservative, laissez-faire-oriented Republicans. The Morgan County Republican Party Charles led for two decades abandoned him in the process.

Thus, Grandfather evolved as he shifted from laissez-faire advocacy, to the reshaping of prior laissez-faire policies, into more progressive government program leadership. Pushback ensued, statewide. Much of it had its genesis with orthodox Mormons who were descendants of polygamist families, Morgan County families included, as well as those extending from the orthodox polygamous families from which Charles Condie and Georgiana Toone were descended.

My Condie grandparents raised six children in Morgan, mainly in a manner that was more secular than it was compliant with Mormon orthodoxy. For instance, only one of the six Condie children pursued a conventional Mormon temple marriage.

Following public service in the Bamberger Administration, and rather than returning to Morgan, Charles and Georgiana settled in the more cosmopolitan railroad town of Ogden, which is the closest railhead to the site where California's governor, Leland Stanford, drove the Golden Spike in 1869. The last phase of Charles's career, as Ogden River water commissioner, led him to collaborate with other water leaders to construct the Willard Spur.

Now, in 2024 however, the Willard Spur is leaking multi-millions of gallons that don't reach or replenish the parched Great Salt Lake. This unfortunate loss of water could be fixed at a cost of perhaps $100 million. The investment could save the daily leakage of 3 million gallons and the seasonal loss of perhaps hundreds of thousands of birds that die because of inadequate water flow into Great Salt Lake's Willard Bay.

Even so, the Legislature's Republican supermajority continues its failure to appropriate sufficient sums to fix this problem. Instead, cultural and political demagoguery, allegedly, continues to be the object of year-after-year right-wing legislative prioritization.

A couple of times during my childhood, in unguarded moments, Melba's sisters reflected on their roots in Morgan County by relying on a black sheep metaphor. Indeed, the family was neither a sheepish family noir, nor a "blanc" one, although a blanc vs. noir metaphor does well-communicate the bifurcated ideological environment in which the family was raised. Mainly, however, the Condie kids grew up clinging to laissez-faire, as evidenced by the governor's office spectacle orchestrated by Melba and supported by siblings Myron and Leona.

So, Mitt. Here's what I believe. I think bullying is part and parcel of what Utah Mormondom was and is about—even now—in my family, throughout Utah, and beyond. Uncle Myron's debacle in the office of Utah's Democratic Governor is testimony to that. And across my life, there has been much family-centric evidence of bullying.

I believe bullying best describes how I became the object of my family's attempted humiliation at the Utah governor's office, in the person of Uncle Myron. My belief is that Uncle Mike, as we called him, and his siblings—Melba included—believed they were bullied or belittled as kids, in Morgan, by the Mormon orthodoxy.

Later, they refined the bullying strategies they believed had been used on them but began using them instead, on various family and community members, me included.

I also believe bullying is an appropriate metaphor to explain dominant political strategies—employed now—especially now—by Utah's legislative Republican super-majority, as recently as 2024.

As Utah goes—I believe—so also goes our nation.

CHAPTER 4: TRUMP DIDN'T DO THIS HIMSELF

YO MITT:

Thomas Edsall, *New York Times* columnist, writes that "Trump Didn't Do It Himself." I add: Donald Trump, a highly focused marketer, has anticipated successfully, how to both lead and how to follow—in the direction of his alt-right-leaning acolytes.

With biography, Edsall compares the presidential elections of 1992 (GHW Bush vs. B Clinton) and 2016 (D Trump vs. H Clinton), through a lens focused on high-authoritarian white voters. In the '92 election these voters went about 50-50 for Republican and Democratic candidates, respectively. Not so, 24 years later. In '16, the year of Trump, high authoritarian white voters supported Republican over Democrat candidates by about a four-to-one margin.

Mitt, interested in when you were "on-stage" in the 2012 presidential contest? Then, this target group went about two to one for you, over Obama.

This dramatic and growing schism described by Edsall has given rise to a "media bastardization" of sorts. MAGA-oriented Republicans, allegedly, tend to be media-portrayed as "obedience-driven," whereas humanist-leaning Democrats tend to be portrayed, instead, as supporters of "emancipatory values" (e.g., civic tolerance; individual self-expression).

So, Mitt, let's look at some factors implicit in this massive 24-year realignment. Edsall cites the work of Rachel Kleinfeld who observes that the Great Recession played a pivotal role.

Whereas the financial crisis created a desire for more government intervention, it also triggered dissatisfaction, she points out, among target group members who favor public redistribution schemes aimed "at the deserving only." Further, says Kleinfeld, this angry and newly mobilized group is better described not as choosing antidemocratic behavior per se, but instead, as "choosing a tribe" with which to affiliate, with whom members share common ground.

Some additional characteristics associated with the Edsall analysis are as follows.

Kleinfeld et. al. highlights the insurrection at our nation's capital on January 6, 2021. Almost half of surveyed, self-described Republicans indicate agreement that "J6 events were patriotic acts." Indeed, almost three-quarters express disapproval regarding the House Select Committee (the "Liz Cheney Committee") that was formed to investigate.

Prediction-wise, as Edsall notes along with Joshua Jackson and Dan Medvedev, seven key topics identify target group members in their marshalling against the emancipatory values espoused by those who are more humanistically oriented. These are justification of homosexuality, euthanasia, divorce, prostitution, suicide, abortion, and failure to enforce child obedience at home and elsewhere.

In sum, Edsall concludes authoritarianism plays an increasingly dominant role in American political judgement, as it tends to move individuals so characterized toward intolerance, consonant with other like-minded individuals. Group members tend to support a worldview of obedience and conformity, as well as the belief that too much emphasis upon diversity and autonomy signals instability and social rebellion.

Generally, these individuals favor traditional over progressive values, and they oppose relaxed standards regarding gender, sexual morality, and immigration. Thus, Edsall asserts, they are also more likely than moderates or liberals to accept authoritarian governance, and to act disdainfully toward attempts to suppress violations of established democratic norms.

Regarding the political platform of Donald Trump, Edsall concludes, his antidemocratic appeals are likely to be received favorably by his audience. Further, his target group members are likely to describe the world about them as danger filled, and to promote their leader as the appropriate political antidote for the dangers they sense.

So here you have it, Mitt. The MAGA-oriented crowd is likely to view J6 insurrectionists as patriots and to condemn moderates and liberals who show empathy for others choosing divorce, abortion, etc., and thus to eschew values of humanism, generally. Ostensibly, target group members may also demonstrate an elevated taste for political bullying, perhaps even to the extent of supporting political violence.

For Mormons, allegedly, high authoritarians are likely to represent themselves as institutionally obedient and socially conforming with other like-minded LDS members, and to adhere to church-centric "laundry lists" of requirements. Subservience allows them to remain, comfortably, in good institutional standing. This includes presenting themselves in continuous compliance with standards for temple eligibility and temple attendance.

Obedience, intolerance, social conformity, strength-based responses to perceived threats, yadda, yadda, yadda (as Jerry Seinfeld might have said!)

As described, Edsall identifies a 24-year span in which white authoritarianism went from playing a moderate role, to a much more dominant one in American politics and culture. French

Theory, as it has come to be known, was imported by liberal academics into American universities, especially in the 1980s. Then, by the 1990's, a counter-revolution was underway among American conservatives. The contours of French Theory offer an insightful roadmap into communication strategies among ideologues of the left and right, particularly as conservative dialogue has segued into what has become the Donald Trump-focused MAGA movement. "Deconstruct" and "reframe" are among the by-words.

Francois Cusset's 2003 masterwork on *French Theory* is summarized by an Amazon reviewer:

> During the last three decades of the twentieth century, a disparate group of radical French thinkers achieved an improbable level of influence and fame in the United States. Compared by at least one journalist to the British rock 'n' roll invasion, the arrival of works by Michel Foucault, Jacques Derrida, Jean-François Lyotard, Jean Baudrillard, Gilles Deleuze, and Félix Guattari on American shores in the late 1970s and 1980s caused a sensation.

Outside the academy, French theory had a profound impact on the era's emerging identity politics while also becoming... the target of right-wing propagandists. At the same time in academic departments across the country, their poststructuralist form of radical suspicion transformed disciplines from literature to anthropology to architecture. By the 1990s, French theory was woven deeply into America's cultural and intellectual fabric.

Regarding right-wing Utah Politics, the *Saint George News* observed the following with regard to the 2024 legislature that wrapped up on March 1:

As the gavel fell on Friday night of the 45-day session,

legislators had passed a whopping 591 bills that included a third year of adding anti-trans-gender legislation, setting aside ample funding for a school voucher alternative to conventional public education, and funding for another round of tax cuts that flow disproportionately to the wealthiest Utahns in the top 1 percent of all earners. They also passed HB 257, a revised definition of "female" and "male" to conform with the status of one's reproductive organs at birth.

Being moderate-to-liberal, the *Salt Lake Tribune* was substantially less tolerant:

The 2024 regular session of the Utah Legislature ended as it began. With an aura of utter arrogance. An attitude that the members of the Republican supermajority know what is best for us and there is no need for them to listen to anyone else.

This patriarchal view is normal for Utah's many anti-intellectual, anti-transparency, anti-empathy-for-the-least-of-these elected officials. But it reached new heights this year. As it seems to every year.

Such an approach to governing could be tolerable, even admirable, if the result were a Legislature with the spine to cut through the confusion, face down the special interests and deal with Utah's most pressing issues.

If these lawmakers would tackle what is, on some days, the nation's worst air quality. The slowly-but-surely dying Great Salt Lake....

Instead, we have a legislative branch that is a maddeningly sterile hybrid of conceit and cowardice.

We are governed by people who cannot or will not help our state move forward because they have no vision, or don't think it is the proper role of government or can't be bothered to find the money to pay for it.

Wow!

For a wrap up regarding Utah's 2024 legislative specifics, see the *Tribune* Bryan Schott et. al.'s post-session analysis, March 2.

◆ ◆ ◆

Below are links to articles on the growth, dominance, and shrinkage of the institutional LDS church, in Utah and beyond, and related impacts:

Mormons account for nearly 90 percent of the state Legislature

Short-term blip or longer trend? Surveys shed light on the LDS Church membership stagnation

How many U.S. Latter-day Saints are in church every week?

New study shows most adults in the state don't identify as members of the predominant faith

One in four U.S. Latter-day Saints has thought about leaving the church

How do members of LDS faith compare to other religions? Let's look at some data.

A recent YouGov poll: LDS finish just behind atheism and Wicca

Deeper findings contain better news and worse news for the LDS Church

Why the explanations for slower LDS Church growth may all be wrong—or right

NPR America at a Crossroads with Judy Woodruff, on religion (video)

Multiple complaints over LDS tithing are rolled into one suit accusing the church of fraud

Utah's LDS vs. non-LDS divide: In and out groups split neighborhoods

CHAPTER 5: MELBA'S MORMON CUDGEL: AGAIN?

YO MITT!

Are you sitting down?

This is a short case history about right-wing authoritarianism, as it operates in Mormondom, and how it came to permeate my marriage and family—disastrously.

I need something like a therapy session, Mitt, if you're "up" for time-traveling back to your Boston period, when you were a volunteer Mormon bishop and stake president. If you're OK with "fantasy-shrinking," that would be just swell, but even better would be this. How about just listening a bit, momentarily?

Sound weird? Perhaps, but here goes. (Of course, this preamble is queued for "affect," and besides, "real" senators are much too busy to take deep dives into these sorts of life events. *Please don't feel obliged to phone, Mitt, really!*)

I feel I'm both a winner and a loser, having grown up Mormon. In many ways my religion became a childhood "ticket" out of the chaos characterizing my birth family, and it worked, at least partially. How else could I have ended up with a PhD and a storybook career, I wonder?

On the downside, however, my life within and without Utah's Mormondom has evolved into what feels like a never-ending downward spiral into the pedantic forces of authoritarianism.

At times, it seemed breakthroughs toward cultural authenticity ("Good Cop") might lie just around the corner. But then "Bad Cop" forces set in, always. That's when it appears the entire Mormon-oriented culture of hopefulness is being swept away, allegedly, by an institutionally motivated counterforce of power-driven orthodoxy.

My hypothesis is this. Power corrupts, and absolute power corrupts, absolutely. Analytically, it's called Michels's Iron Law of Oligarchy. I believe, allegedly, that in the hands of highly orthodox Mormon authoritarians, institutional forces win, virtually always, over those oriented toward more humanistic outcomes.

What's the solution then, Mitt, when at times it appears impossible to survive and thrive, amid rigid Mormon authoritarianism and other similar, highly controlling systems of religion and politics? I believe it is this.

Avoid feigning institutional piety. Tell the truth, to oneself especially. Marshal one's interior forces authentically. Live for outcomes rather than wishes, merely. Go one's way—even to pursue paths untrod—leading...hopefully...to "new game plans" for challenging whatever lies around the next bend in the road.

When it may become necessary, why not strike out on one's own, as *NY Times* columnist David French did, as he describes in "My Old Church Canceled Me."

Mother was mentally ill, episodically—with bipolar disorder—and she resisted attempts by Buss to help moderate her-at-times-bizarre behaviors within the family. Even so, Melba cultivated a teaching career in special education and demonstrated then-successful abilities—during the 1960s and 1970s—to "structure" students experiencing "behavioral challenges."

The bashing I took at the hands of Myron and Marjorie, at the

Utah capitol, could not have occurred without Melba's complicity. Then, about five years later, a second "Melba takedown" occurred. The first time, Kay was aware of Melba's chicanery. The second, however, my spouse became a family co-protagonist, allegedly, in what felt like an ultimate "let's get Jimmy" ruse. It happened, commensurate with relocating to Corvallis, Oregon, where I was assuming a new academic job.

Previously, and immediately following our Salt Lake City stint, I worked at West Virginia University in Morgantown. However, with the sudden death of Kay's father, I sought to support her through our relocation to be closer, geographically, to her widowed mother.

About the time we were in transit to Corvallis, as Melba later recounted, mother had a chance encounter at a family reunion in Utah with Corvallis relatives. They were Mildred, Melba's long-lost niece, and Paul, Mildred's husband. Paul, a professor at Oregon State University, was also the Mormon bishop in the Corvallis ward into which we were about to take up geographic residence, coincidently.

Along with renewing her relationship with Mildred, Melba later described to me how she responded to Paul, upon learning of his ecclesial bishop's role. "Help him! Please help Jim and Kay, his wife!"—she implored.

Wow. "Melba One" had precipitated Myron's debacle at the Utah governor's office. Now, "Melba Two's about-to-hatch debacle" pointed toward yet another off-the-rails-attempt to reform me. My "crime," according to Melba? Being outspoken in favor of moderate and liberal causes.

Immediately, Corvallis became synonymous for me with church-oriented dustups. It spelled trouble, allegedly, because Kay also "set me up, opportunistically," consistent with Melba's attempt to "mess" with my life and career. By then, of course, I was no longer a dependent adolescent but married, with two kids and a mortgage.

Upon relocating, Kay immediately established rapport with Mildred and Paul. Consequently, it appeared that details of our family life were filtering from Kay to Mildred, and then on to Bishop Paul. Privacy? Not much. Presumably also, information about me was "lubricating" Bishop Paul's evolving plan regarding his apparent pledge to support what he believed Melba wanted. But did Melba and Paul want the same thing? Probably not. Although conservative, Melba was not a right-wing authoritarian ideologue, per se.

Train wreck forthcoming? You bet.

I found Paul to be a highly traditional authoritarian Mormon male with highly specific sex role views, allegedly. His political ideology, ostensibly, aligned with his orthodox religious views. Those who wish might consult BYU's Tim Heaton and his "Four C's of the Mormon Family: Chastity, Conjugality, Children, and Chauvinism," or Mormon leader Ezra Benson's "What Manner of Men Ought We to Be? (video)."

As we established ourselves in Corvallis, I perceived that Kay was continuing in her emulation of the families of various orthodox Mormon friends. I believe she grieved about inadequacies in her family of origin and perhaps fantasized, allegedly, about what it would have been like to have been raised as a so-called "Molly Mormon," instead. As she sought to strengthen bonds with her friends, she also commiserated with them about her perceptions of my "foot dragging." It was about her quest to live more harmoniously with her perceived Mormonness, and my reluctance to meet her fully in the space she envisioned.

◆ ◆ ◆

Allegedly, the closer Kay drew to Mildred and Paul, the more strident and hate-filled she became toward me. Eventually, I learned that based solely on Kay's input, Bishop Paul was marshaling a case against me, aimed at church excommunication. Kay's charges, via Bishop Paul, apparently included sexual and physical abuse.

I consulted Pete, my older brother, who fancied himself as our Mormon family patriarch, about how I was being "set up" by Bishop Paul, and what I could do to counter the situation. His view? Stay securely in the "good graces" of your bishop, he advised. In the finality of eternal judgements, Pete observed, Paul's pronouncements, as your bishop and your judge, may bring down God's eternal judgment upon you.

Wow. That didn't sound like anything germinating from the birth family in which we were co-raised. Our father was antagonistic toward institutional Mormonism, and during most of my growing up years, mother was a disconnected nonattender. Whatever.

As time passed, I felt Kay was continuing to broadcast to her friends that her marriage partner was inadequate as a Mormon husband. For instance, following divorce, while visiting Salt Lake City, I recall a department store encounter with a former church colleague and friend. It did not go well. He responded to me, I sensed, as though I had somehow devolved into something akin to a moral "leper." Therefore, presumably, I had become someone to be carefully avoided. Allegedly, did Kay have a direct or indirect hand in this and perhaps other social "meltdowns," I wonder?

I have described encounters such as this as "soft bullying." In Amish communities, similar behavior is called shunning. In Mormon as well as other authoritarian communities, it leads—often—to hard bullying, or worse.

Finally, our marriage crisis came to a head—a second time—following an event that occurred when we resided in Salt Lake City, a couple of years earlier. Then, Kay had withdrawn all our funds, surreptitiously, from a joint bank account used primarily to save for a house downpayment. Allegedly, she turned the balance—in toto—over to a lawyer, who held it in escrow for a "divorce on demand," she later told me, after I had discovered the charade when I attempted a bank withdrawal to pay monthly bills. Later, before moving from Salt Lake City, Kay replaced the money.

Next, in Corvallis, Kay was leaving the impression with our home teachers, allegedly, that our marriage was about to "boil over." They were counseling regularly with Bishop Paul, also, about the Sawyer family, but were in broad disagreement with the bishop regarding causes of discord in our home. Allegedly, they saw Kay as the provocateur. Apparently also, they were becoming aware that Bishop Paul was contemplating my excommunication, entirely upon misinformation, allegedly, he had been gleaning from Kay.

Oh, from where Melba began only months earlier, what damage she was inciting, again!

Ultimately, the home teachers contacted the stake president and asked him to assume institutional responsibility, rather than the bishop, for counseling Kay and Jim. Soon, we received an invitation from the stake president.

He was ideologically moderate and met with us as a couple, several times over several weeks, with counseling sessions lasting at least one hour each. Timewise, his commitment was extraordinary.

Eventually, he asked me to meet with him privately. Then, he inquired if I would be divorcing Kay, and if so, allegedly, for me to move quickly for the wellbeing of our sons, rather than to drag out family conflict, further. He also asked my consent for him to recommend me to the bishop of the new Seattle ward into which I would be moving. I consented. Earlier, I had explained that I was being recruited to join the faculty at Seattle University.

Next, I filed for divorce and began searching for Seattle housing. The apartment I chose was in a predominant student ward, geographically close to the University of Washington. Following my move, I checked with the university research physician who was next to become my Mormon bishop, geographically. That's when I received an unexpected "hero's welcome" of sorts, based apparently upon an eloquent recommendation to the bishop, forwarded from the Corvallis stake president.

Immediately, I was called as the permanent Sunday school instructor for young adults and young marrieds, known as the gospel doctrine class, including with mentoring responsibilities. Simultaneously, I accepted an assignment to mentor a 14-year-old girl, as her practice partner, as she prepared for a dance recital. And most significantly, I accepted a church calling to home teach and mentor the woman who had been Ted Bundy's long-standing partner, and her daughter, at the home where they had lived with the serial murderer who also became a Mormon convert. At that time, Bundy was temporarily jailed in Colorado, although eventually he was executed in Florida's electric chair.

Thus, beginning in Corvallis, I went from facing excommunication under the regime of an alt-right Mormon bishop who was acting solely, allegedly, on Kay's cognizance, to receiving a leadership calling at the stake level, only about four months after my Seattle arrival. Absolutely amazing! I retained the existing church jobs but declined the stake leadership position because my calendar was fast approaching overload.

Mitt, an introduction to Kay is in order. We met in a psychology class at Weber State University, several months following my return from being a mission volunteer in New Zealand. Our relationship got off to a buoyant start, including with mutually and enthusiastically embraced petting (a Mormon no-no for those aspiring to temple marriage), and then Kay invited me to accompany her on a brief professional visit with a psychiatrist she had scheduled through the university. Her rationale? Allegedly, she was attempting to break a childhood thumb-sucking habit.

Turns out, apparently the "shrink" who the university selected for her believed in "pseudo-science fantasies" associated with Sigmund Freud. He limited her appointment to 30 minutes as he concluded that her habit would abate with marriage.

He was alluding, apparently, as per Freud, that her evolving interest in a new husband's penis would replace her interest in her thumb. Lame! Really lame! The psychiatrist made no inquiry into possible childhood trauma, tragically. All around, his advice was short-sighted and very unprofessional, I believe.

Kay encountered more bad psychological advice, latter-on, with counseling visits near Corvallis, that I undertook with her at Bishop Paul's request. The new shrink, who Paul recommended and favored highly, was little more than a right-wing authoritarian ideologue, doubling as Bishop Paul's alter ego, I perceived.

Early on, in Ogden, following Kay's short psychiatric interview, we talked at length. She filled in blanks about her childhood. Her family life had been unstable, allegedly, owing to traumatic life events. As an infant, while crawling unattended on the floor, she pierced an eye on a sharp object and became fully blinded in that eye, permanently. About that time, her slightly older brother drowned, following his wandering away at a picnic, streamside, unattended by his parents. Years later, as a middle schooler, Kay watched through her parents' picture window as a utility worker died in their front yard in a trench cave-in barely 30 feet from her.

Perhaps, as a psychology major with well-developed empathic skills, Kay sensed in me the opportunity to collaborate on building a solid marital foundation. It did not evolve that way, however.

◆ ◆ ◆

My hypothesis? Kay fantasized, allegedly, about living in a family without manifold trauma, that had been triggered in her family of origin by lackadaisical parenting. What she craved was to fantasy-relive her childhood, I believe, but guided by orthodox Mormon parents instead of the ones to which she had been "assigned." Additionally, following our temple marriage, Kay carried guilt about Mormon-forbidden petting, apparently.

Dating a former missionary appeared promising, perhaps, but was I the right one? Allegedly, she came to view me—a budding intellectual—as someone pulling her further from Mormon "pie-in-the-sky authoritarianism" about which she seemed to fantasize.

As an undergraduate major in psychology, with lots of career-wise applied counseling experience, I'm confident of this. The path to finding closure in one's life—especially following profound childhood trauma such as Kay experienced—lies solely with the development of authenticity, engaged from within. Allegedly, that's not the path Kay pursued, however. Instead, she turned outward rather than inward, to scapegoat me.

Therapy-wise, what was needed, I believe, was a competent, ethically professional therapist, rather than just another right-wing authoritarian ideologue.

About six weeks into marriage, we experienced our first physical encounter following another failed lovemaking session. I believe Kay was relying on the psychiatrist's bogus assessment, allegedly, that her husband would somehow cure her addiction, and by association, most everything else, sexually and otherwise. Then, an hour later, while seated at our kitchen table for a meal, Kay slapped me across my face, allegedly, precipitously and without provocation. What a surprise!

When confronted years later, in one of our joint interviews with the Corvallis stake president, Kay asserted, allegedly, she slapped me because she had just been raped by me. I presume she also made a similar claim to Bishop Paul and that he was incorporating it into the case he was building for my excommunication, also known as "membership withdrawal."

Obviously, the stake president did not accept her assertion and concluded, allegedly, that her slap coincided with a release of frustration regarding unresolved sexual issues, likely based upon unresolved childhood traumas.

From this place at our marriage's beginning, allegedly, Kay's level of hatred rose episodically, I recall vividly. A few weeks later, in another confrontation in which she hatefully disavowed her joint responsibility with me to seek resolution of our marital conflict, I returned the slap. It was a serious mistake and one deeply regretted. It represented immaturity on my part, as well as hers. It also played into allegations Kay made to Bishop Paul, allegedly, that she was being abused sexually and physically, and as such, that I was dishonoring my temple-contracted Mormon priesthood obligations. Those contract-like religious obligations are also described or implied in the Heaton and Benson links, pertinent to "chauvinism" and to "What manner of men ought we to be? (video)"

Allegedly, mutual shoving and slapping continued intermittently, until abruptly, Kay stopped. Allegedly, her hatred toward me did not.

Below are links illuminating the relationship between passive or "soft bullying" and potentially aggressive "hard bullying." Here, the context, primarily, is Mormon sex role expectations and requirements; particularly those evolving around institutional attempts to reelevate behavioral standards for Mormon garment-wearing by temple eligible women, particularly:

Gospel Answers Every Doubt and Faith Challenge, Elder Cook Tells Young Adults

How the discipline of six dissidents continues to trouble the Mormon church

30 years after the 'September Six' purge, would the LDS Church do

it again?

Writer excommunicated during 'September Six' purge loses her bid to rejoin the LDS Church

BYU's new hires face a new hurdle

List of revised temple recommend questions

Three decades ago Elder Packer warned against feminists, homosexuals and intellectuals

LDS Church steps up this message: Wear your temple garments every day

The Wearing—or not wearing—of LDS garments is personal and should stay that way

LDS garments: From urinary tract and yeast infections to period, pregnancy, afterbirth, nursing, and menopause needs....

LDS women no longer meet separately with a designated apostle

Does the Mormon Church Empower Women?

When did the rules about women working outside the home change?

Breaking down the gender wage gap in Utah

The Gender Pay Gap Is a Culture Problem

CHAPTER 6: POST-SCRIPTS

YO MITT: MISFEASANCE IN MORMONDOM?

Kay was <u>not</u> an ideologue, as was Bishop Paul. Rather, I believe she acted opportunistically, not unlike the way Melba acted toward me near the end of her life. Fortunately, Mitt, the Melba-Paul-Kay triad ran itself "off the rails." Even so, the resulting damage led to severe and unintended consequences.

One consequence—I speculate—was perhaps revealed in Paul's untimely death—only a few years afterward. I guesstimate he died perhaps two decades prematurely, and I wonder. Might cognitive dissonance—related, allegedly, to the fallacious church-family scheme over which he attempted to preside—have been a factor?

A second Mormon bishop's death in this scam-saturated bruhaha occurred as well. Bruce, then a newly minted Seattle area bishop, attempted to help me and my sons, postdivorce, altruistically. Tragically, he died also, abruptly. Could a factor in his untimely death have been stress related, allegedly, due to the "Corvallis scam" that overloaded profoundly his calendar commitments?

More follows, Mitt, on the two deaths.

Church-wise, my life in Seattle was integrity affirming, but at enormous human costs. Consequently, I wonder. Rather than a huge negative, might the Kay-Paul-nexus have ended instead, as a positive, perhaps something like this?

What if Kay's appeal for church help had led toward this end? Rather than responding as a deep alt-right Mormon ideologue, what if Bishop Paul had responded instead by referring her to a competent, ethical and nonideologically aligned psychologist? That is, what if he had connected her with someone skilled in dealing with the sort of severe childhood traumas Kay had endured?

Regarding failed outcomes, a knowledgeable university colleague with multiple Mormon contacts and no "ax to grind," observes this. No one has survived church-related rebuke of the intensity I experienced in Corvallis. What seems typical is this. If someone turns publicly critical of their Mormon affiliation, they are likely to "perish" institutionally as they watch their Mormon marriage, family life, and even church-related friendships dissolve around them.

Doctrinairely, the implicit LDS promise is if someone honors their religion, they will "prosper," regardless. However, I call it Pete's edict, adjusted for consistency with my experience, and it is sarcastic, unfortunately. Stay on your Mormon bishop's "good" side, it argues. Otherwise, if he renders negative judgements about you, your outcome may be nothing less than God's eternal judgment.

A priest colleague was fond of referring to Catholicism as something akin to the "31 ice cream flavors of Baskin-Robbins." What he meant was this. If you want to remain Catholic but don't favor the Jesuit order, then why not try another of the many "31-plus flavors," such as the Franciscans or Benedictines, for instance. They're all "ice cream," of course, but each order is flavored somewhat uniquely.

Preeminently and to the contrary however, there is only a single flavor in Mormonism. There are no second, third or fourth alternatives from which to choose. When "push comes to shove," the only thing that likely remains "on the table" perennially is this: high authoritarian orthodoxy. Ultimately, in situations such as mine, "good cop" interventions, allegedly, are virtually certain to be replaced—eventually—by "bad cop" recriminations.

Mitt, do you remember the prominent Pogo cartoon by Walt Kelly, from the Vietnam War era? "We have met the enemy, and the enemy is us," was the essence of Kelly's insightfulness. Amid devastating conflict, even as we may become party to inflicting "hell" upon our perceived enemies, Kelly's "strip" asserts that it is us—solely and ultimately—who "call ourselves to account" for whatever our "sins" may be.

Indeed, when we act "enemy-like," then we become more likely to perceive ourselves, eventually, as "the enemy." Conscience matters. For instance, how often may suicide result from a "self-immolation-type action" such as Kelly's cartoon envisions?

As a former police department volunteer, I have attended suicide "clean-ups," and my opinions are strong. Allegedly, I also attempted to mentor my second wife's cousin, at the request of my spouse and her family. Gail's cousin was a Vietnam war veteran and assured me frequently, he was complicit in "unspeakable crimes against humanity."

Al returned from war with only one leg. One night, amid his deeply felt angst, Al took his life by shooting his only good leg, and then immobilizing himself while he bled out in the cab of his truck. His family found him the next morning, just steps away from where they had been sleeping.

How might Walt Kelly's words apply now, as the 2024 presidential election approaches? Thomas Edsall offers insight. Donald Trump didn't accomplish contemporary America's divisionism and hatefulness, alone. Rather, he had help: lots of help. If we are honest about a prime cause, it lies within many of us, I believe, as Pogue cartoonist Kelly might have asserted.

Allegedly, our contemporary problem may not be so much about leaders acting in roles reminiscent of authoritarian gargoyles swooping down from the cathedrals you envision, Mitt. Thanks for a great metaphor, however. But I submit, instead, the primal American problem has become this. It's not so much about authoritarian leadership, but rather, it's about authoritarian followership.

That's right. In Mormondom particularly, the prime problem—I believe—is this. As Kleinfeld states, it's about the newly angry and newly mobilized, and how their choice of a "tribe" of like-minded people determines affiliation, and with it, ideology.

So, what to do about it? I suggest beginning with two simple rules, applied by—and for—all of us, Mormons and non-Mormons alike: here, there, and everywhere.

> Rule One: In public spaces such as city council or school board meetings, use the term "I know" sparingly, when "I believe" may be more appropriate, and honest.

> Rule Two: In place of the pursuit of unmitigated self-interest, substitute instead, the pursuit of self-interest, "rightly understood."

That is, act less in citizen roles related to being—merely—a consumer of government-provided services, such as Social Security or Medicaid. Instead, act more "civically" in roles related to "responsible citizen." President "Jack" Kennedy described this well during the 1960s. "Ask not what your country can do for you, but ask instead, what you can do for your country."

Indeed, ask this. How may our respective contributions improve the common good?

◆ ◆ ◆

In the era of Donald Trump and MAGA, allegedly, America's massive problem has become one of sliding ever further, from authoritarianism, into fascism. Indeed, authoritarianism and fascism come down to one and the same, eventually.

According to former Trump communications director Anthony Scaramucci, "If you understand fascism, you have a five-alarm bell going off in your head." Or as George Mason professor Tehama Bunyasi cautions, "The American people should beware any candidate that does not rebuke these three outright: 'Nazism, imperialism, and dictatorship'."

Former Secretary of State Madeline Albright was explicit about how authoritarianism and fascism are one and the same, ultimately. As many as a dozen of Albright's relatives, in Czechoslovakia—including three of her grandparents—were murdered in the Holocaust.

How to escape authoritarianism, aka fascism? In Mormondom, one might begin by challenging—personally—the far-too-frequent community focus on moral minutia. For instance, what about starting with personal reflections on one's piousness?

Mormon author Stephen Covey encouraged his readers to avoid placing "perception above reality." Alternately stated, don't fulfill the so-called "letter of the law," while overlooking, simultaneously, the intent for which it was promulgated.

For some, why not begin by interrogating Mormon temple recommend questions, the answers one gives, and the motivation. Matthew 23:23 offers a vital clue, allegedly, about how to prioritize effectively, and how to avoid pedanticism.

Woe unto you, scribes and Pharisees, hypocrites! for ye pay tithe of mint and anise and cummin, and have omitted the weightier matters of the law, judgment, mercy, and faith: these ought ye to have done, and not to leave the other undone. King James Version.

James (Jim) Sawyer

James E. (Jim) Sawyer holds a PhD in economics from the University of Utah and has held academic appointments at West Virginia, Oregon State and Seattle Universities, Fulbright Fellowships in France and Portugal, a joint appointment with French Universite du Littoral Cote d' Opale, and a Visiting Scholar appointment with the Nord Pas de Calais Regional Council.

In the United States, Jim held administrative and academic appointments including an endowed chair, served as advisor to a Utah Governor, taught graduate courses in finance, economic theory and organization theory, and undergraduate courses in political economy, organization leadership and civic engagement.

In Colorado, Jim produced public affairs radio programming. He writes extensively on topics related to economic doctrines, ethics, civics, moral development, and theology. He is published in France, Belgium, the United States, and Great Britain where Jim was represented in a macroeconomic paradigm challenge by the London publisher (Macmillan) that represented JM Keynes in JMK's doctrinal challenge to conventional theories about the causes and consequences of the Great Depression.

Jim served on the Board of World Wisdoms Project aka Northern

Colorado Theologian in Residence Project. He is emeritus from Seattle University.